Kill-site

BOOKS BY TIM LILBURN

POETRY

Names of God (1986)
From the Great Above She Opened Her Ear to the Great Below
(with Susan Shantz) (1988)
Tourist to Ecstasy (1989)
Moosewood Sandhills (1994)
To the River (1999)
Kill-site (2003)

ESSAYS

Poetry and Knowing: Speculative Essays and Interviews (editor) (1995)
Living in the World as if It Were Home (1999)
Thinking and Singing: Poetry and the Practice of Philosophy (editor) (2002)

Kill-site

TIM LILBURN

M&S

National Library of Canada Cataloguing in Publication

Lilburn, Tim, 1950-
Kill-site / Tim Lilburn.

Poems.
ISBN 0-7710-5321-5

I. Title.

PS8573.I427K54 2003   C811'.54   C2002-905715-9
PR9199.3.L514K54 2003

We acknowledge the financial support of the Government of Canada through the Book Publishing Industry Development Program and that of the Government of Ontario through the Ontario Media Development Corporation's Ontario Book Initiative. We further acknowledge the support of the Canada Council for the Arts and the Ontario Arts Council for our publishing program.

Typeset in Minion by M&S, Toronto
Printed and bound in Canada

McClelland & Stewart Ltd.
The Canadian Publishers
481 University Avenue
Toronto, Ontario
M5G 2E9
www.mcclelland.com

6 7 8 9 10   07 06 05 04

No, it's not a migraine but the cold of genderless space.

— OSIP MANDELSTAM

... and I, drawing from beside my thigh my sharp sword,
dug a pit, of about a cubit in each direction,
and poured it full of drink offerings for the dead, first
honey mixed with milk, and the second pouring was sweet wine,
and the third, water, and over it all I sprinkled white barley.

— *ODYSSEY* XI: 24-28

CONTENTS

I

II

III

I

Corn-coloured, stroked movement, a dark brown of choosing
sailing it forward, the animal came near the round roofed willow
hut, bees stabbing along the pollen-knuckled dome;
the animal curved to the place that breathed apart, on its own,
                            its breath circling it like a moon,
and lodged itself in the deep water of wintered-over leaves,
            where an ear scouted, spining the leaves with a throaty blue light.
The animal came plumed and choired with night.
It is here.
It fell forward on an unseeably black, under-all-radars, eaten boat,
                    a rib for a mast.
It travelled below the ground, it came from a hole in the yellow hill.
There was no Jesuit baroque, no chest-grab for Europe.
The animal's hearing had a rod-on, at the end of it a first quarter moon,
the animal thought and one plum-black, inch-deep stream
flowed under glacial till 800 yards.
In my ear the mauve smell wolves like   in my mouth
night and deeper night
pulling down from waiting.
In the animal's undelivered speech was perhaps the burn-whiskered
            cross of Chimayo.
The animal was the world; it was the world.

3

Bareback Quill Lakes country in tamping snow, colour of a
Sportsman cigarette tin, then drifting, almost Christmas, roads about to
close, nothing coming out of the ground, greed with teeth eats me,
distance or Christic loneliness eats me.
A blue city under the snow – its name is Unending, or, in another
    language, Hardly There.   Pine splinters tied into its hair, hanging.
First philosophy is mystical theology.
The fox moves quickly on the snow.
I mean doodling out the taupe-green
lynx spoor of always wanting, which is the single archive of what is
said beyond the wall, the one track into the second world.

Now.
Let the object build weight in the meadow of your eye,
                      because you're not good for much else.

A day's travel southwest, the creased hills fat-walk down to the
Estuary ferry, lifted to the sand above the dark-hoarding ice,
rich, covert, kingly ice, and to the west Big Bear's
eyed hill and the Hutterite colony,
small snow down the slopes, the Red Deer locked, crooked,
ankle-broke, old night coming into its wounds.
Cranberries staining snow, signs of rabbit kill in the excitedly knotted,
breathed world of the elm thicket,
thick back of essence, flab-pleated with omnia, everywhere
opening its seeing-perfumed fist.

4

My first hunched sleep, my
first low ear – low, low, listening smelling like tree moss
thawing in January – are for the dark curl, stubbed
thunder mourning under the chokecherry thicket, nubbly
insistently not-there wind, whose great belly *is* the chokecherry thicket, the
black fountaining of its fed and pleased haecceity – descended ear-sleep,
it is quickly for that one slow thing whose girthy –
it is multi-stomached – hairy-armed waiting,
its stay-in-place waiting, makes for the right arm
of the as-I-am thicket, it builds the arm of the thicket, unfolds
right up to it – so my house is melancholy, so my
house is a musical loneliness.
He said, he said, said to those standing, watching ones.
He said, that is, to Nicholas of Cusa and to Mechthild of Magdeburg.

The far-from-light song goes on inside
the undayed mounds, the in-held lifts, flowing, over miles,
                                        wearing distant silver;
there's a webby smell of turquoise around it and the
rustle of ochre, and, yes, the lightly body odoured
high-shoulderedness of European thought.
Let it go, you think, the sound slim in the diesel smell of the cold.
The sun is a low quake in the forest –
try to find its tail-track in the snow.

Nicholas of Cusa goes down there to meet it, the healed-over sound.
All that comes, he thinks, I will kiss.
Paul Celan flickers down. Cusanus heard something on that long
boat trip from Asia Minor where he was half burnt up, and he's been
dead a long time, so this would suit him. He goes down to meet this
black singing, its darkest seeing.
                              He carries a palm of salt.
Light falls like meltwater under the earth.
I'm on a useless horse nearby, I'm in a collapsed boat in wild camomile,
and I can hear it too, the endless, eyeless mouth,
but it keeps breaking up. Elegantly forgetting itself.
The singing of books sunk in the gummed hills,
the bank buck down to Wolverine Creek, as Benedict said. Hear it
and say it again, say it again.

The animal dreamed of me,
a brown gust separating above its head;
this was below snowhumps on the creek,
ice fog up the towers along
the valley sides, blood on the snow,
estrus marks, the water frozen a yard down.

When Henry Kelsey died or left
Hudson Bay, there's a rumour he continued walking under the ground
in the highest part of his voice, down the west hip of the Porcupine Hills,
a pythagorean veer in his eyes.
Because all this was a new music, uncooked ratio, a machine of smoke.
And he thought   *Let the will sleep here 400 years.*
Let the will sleep here 400 years.
Only some song would turn the lock.
He was looking for the deeper Crees, the Poets, south people sleeping
        along the rock ledges behind their eyes, someone to put something
                                in his mouth.

And because he was under the ground, everything came to him – he
saw a face of wheat, a face
of mineral beam, nipples of stones, a face
of winter in things, face of what is

at the back, the watery, the alto part of the mind,
showing through skin.
(It rose to the skin
      for its hump to be seen, then moved back into the trees.)
Only a song would turn the lock.
He kept walking, wanting and fearing
      the freezing of rivers.

Sandhills in a light, likely daylong rain, looking off
    to the left, grass that's not going anywhere, September – everything walks
toward you; it undresses and comes
                    toward you with its small bright hands
and the downwind smell of your father's mind
and his shoulders in the early summer of 1964;
he's working two jobs, post office, moving company, right
now he's not wearing a shirt, a hundred and forty-five pounds,
but still less under the name of his lower-in-the-throat citizenship,
where he's not saying a thing, living in a cave two-
thirds up a cliff line, how
did he get there, swallows heaving in front of his face, the hole
trench-shovelled into clay sides lifting over the Milk River, north of
the Sweetgrass Hills, cattle clouding off infinitely
to the east, feathers
and bones hung from string at the mouth of the cave,
pale green feathers smooth out long and speechless from his tailbone.
Things climb out of the elms of their names and themselves
and they come forward, moving their tattooed, Fulani hands.
They smell of your father's voice, his
    one
      black
        suit.

Winter now; heavy twist and giving up of snow;
it slump-hulks in from west of the river out of a greenish,
balls-kicked cloud, then sleepwalks down the valley through the
muscle of four thousand cranes, the light of their red foreheads;
if it knew anything, it would be the deepest human voice,
or a little more, three or four throat-singings hanging from fishing wire
104 storeys down the invisible centre of it.
Its sweep and wound are the complete lack of choice.
Now the rilled flank: set this beside the corpus dionysiacum.
Gather me into your forgetting,
cloud the colour of the watch-face my father carried through
Italy, Holland, forty-three, forty-five. Gather me home
into the attention, the float and the visitations and
the bright room. You've seen the mountains
beyond their names
and been seen by them.

❖

The animal that came to me was big with wounds, songful
    with wounds' clatter, with the clatter of wounds.
It wore a dark sound.
It moved into the back country of winter after it lay near my head.
It didn't leave anything, no sachet, no cupped list of names.
Then it went into the bush country of winter.
I don't know what it wanted, it could hardly breathe.
I couldn't breathe.
There was the breath-thunder of snowgeese flyways.

There was *The Evidential Power of Beauty.*
Nothing in the animal's mouth, no neumes, no number chain of sounds,
nothing added to the general name of things that are and those
that are not.
Maybe it meant sleep in some buried clothes
in the hobo jungle by the river that went through Spokane, WA,
in the early eighties, Reagan just elected, a few of us reading
Marx in a small room, crawl back into that, maybe not. That river, then.
The animal smelled of unmixed space.

Sandbars, early November, light-quake on the front of my body.
Cranes
    gone
      almost
        completely.

———————————————

The animal dreamed of me.
It held a ball of light.
   This had been embedded in its burnt-birch, split shoulder
but now was just above its head, shifting, gathering its sea legs.
                    November leaf smell in the light.

All that I had done had set up camp
under the ground,
a lame fire, chewed pot, a blanket smouldering.
Tonight Henry Kelsey would serve
creamed shoe leather and the green backs of stones.
Keep going.

Dogwood leaves amnesiac, religious, turned to the wall;
crickets heavy-shouldered in the fall field that is growing inside the candle
in the tight, stone-lit church, lifted blue and rose from the ground, where
Bernard of Clairvaux is giving his third sermon on the Song of Songs –
the rubble-backed soul breaking off smokily from the moon of the Word,
the guttural rubble of knees and eyes cruising out from the Kiss, The Kiss,
the body tulipping-out, coughing and stumbling –
crickets widening and drying the hammered, low field inside the candle
beside Bernard's glasslike, horse-flanked mouth,
crickets widening, widening the field and deep day.
Bernard mentions the secrecy of the summer of 1964,
my father in a sleeveless t-shirt working for movers after the
6:00 to 3:00 shift at the post office, this is the stag on the hill, the beloved,
let him kiss me with the kiss of his mouth;
he's looking up now and there are bird shadows slamming
        across his cheek and throat, then later, in his seeing, a dark
sucking appears a little to his left, which is not the grave, but
a bunching and rucking of emptiness which he feels mostly under his tongue,
where he appears to see it best, like memory.
This is the war.
Cranes on the river now, their calls small
charges in the upper arm.
Everything is here, everything is inside speech.
        All blood is pooling.
The flats are voice-old,
        one crumbling stroke on a sightless, bull violin. Olderwinter soon,
older   winter. Come quickly if you are coming.

_____

The animal dreamed of me
– smoke of looking namelessly lifting –
below snowbanks on the creek,
ice fog up the towers along
the valley sides, blood on the snow,
estrus marks along the water frozen a yard down,
then the kill-site around the next bend.
But the animal moving, breathing,
who dreamed, let go on a wind of not-its-own thinking.

Henry Kelsey died or left
Hudson Bay, but then started walking under the ground
in the highest part of his voice, walking under
the ground, down the west shoulder of the Porcupine Hills,
a pythagorean shake and jump in his eyes.
All this was a new music, blindfolded ratio, a milk-bunting machine of
            smoke, and he was just beginning to see how it bellied out.
And he thought   *Let the will sleep here 400 years.* Let it go down in
the grass.   *Let the will sleep here 400 years.*
Only some song would turn the lock.
He was looking for the deeper Crees, the sand-coloured, someone to put
            something in his mouth.

And because he was under the ground, everything
entered from the top of his head – a face of wheat, a face
of mineral beam, nipples of stones, a face
of winter in things, a face of what is

14

at the back, the watery, the alto part of the mind,
showing through skin.
He could grunt this for a while, bone twisting on bone along
      his spine-top, the things could crawl forward
         in the body of a single eye, a little
                   eye.
Only a song would turn the lock. He was walking, wanting and fearing
the freezing of rivers.

I see Jan Wyers and Andy Suknaski swaying, alone,
deep in their shacks, skirts flowing, bad fires in their heads,
carried wobbling on mirrored plates, the men touching
their days-apart crotches, sizing up the long Tibetan hair blowing
inside things they never had any idea
they would see, diamond willow, pipestone.
(The hair moving like horses from beneath frothing Pontic crowns.)
The hair moans to them, something not-them in their armpits,
            in the thickness of their torsos wants to crawl under the door
                        toward it.
The hills open, they close.
No one in the beer parlour would put up with this.
Suknaski and Wyers could get beat up for this.
They take what they're thinking and hook it to the wall.
The April snow leans this way, toward us, trying to read our books
through the old overcast of writing, it caves this way
but doesn't fall, it is like a pig of gas,
white, rust-scraped, dragging around in the box of an unlit moving truck.
The bluebirds yesterday were what could be the beginning of sickness
                        in the eye.
The hair makes Wyers and Suknaski think they will stretch out, lose feathers,
    regrow them dangerously, enter the before-room name of the unnamed
                        name.
The hair, or itching, or bald, animal singing, far under hearing, down
where the aquifers are

puts part of them out, then en-gods the rest.
And I think, too, because I'm moving this way, of that open-all-winter
water at the mouth of Beaver Creek, I kept seeing it, seeing it,
nudging into the South Saskatchewan,
magpie prints lipping the snowed ice around it, hello, hello, hello,
hello – red willow, smoky zero music, loneliness
standing in front of the light, holiness, great pulling,
whatever you are, with a face like Sonny Liston,
that lazy murderer.

In the Sunset Motel in Senlac, Saskatchewan, it's possible
to think of *The Spiritual Canticle* with the ear of García Lorca
inside it like a silver imaginary bird. Look at the eyes in the chimed,
sound-locked garden of the poem. They are wolverines twisting back
into heavy poplar, twisting back, waving back.
Possible to dream of the dangerous nun just off the plane from
                    Guatemala who asks to borrow a pair of your shorts.
Turn over this world and there is another world,
            rain clouds hunking through, mind light slabbing like surf
                                around the articulate not-speaking of stone.
Socrates was not an anti-rationalist; his earlier sugar-eye for science, his
small milk lunges, is sublated not abandoned, but he believes a particular
                                                            pose
of knowing drives the car right through the wall though
it may *appear* to be philosophy.
The bad bearing wobble of coyotes' voices just as night begins,
the thorny crown of coyotes with a twin below the ground.
A swallowed percussion of moon on rained-on snow in fenced stubble
going up the hill at the west edge of town,
the dish with its bolts popped out beside the singlewide motel.
Beside this world is another world.
Geese are back but out of sight, moving on green-purple, saline ice,
the April frog sound of natural gas kicking
up in the thigh-big water heater in room 15, rig smell of the carpet, wool

18

sock rig smell of the bath mat, sheets toenail sliced dust,
the moon in the socket of the ear.
It's better to be forgotten. No one ever gets around to saying this.
Better to live in a place like Winter, Sask., for
instance, though this is hard to think.
The mind of St. John of the Cross hovers through you
like a big fish; it bends, lit, in wall-like water its one muscle into a
half-circle and comes back, bends and returns.
Mule deer, bluebirds, the moon instead of a dish.
Phenoxy herbicides enter the extra-cellular fluids like
a small family leaving a station wagon, carrying stiff objects
for a picnic into the grass by the stream. The family is
nameless gathering between the moony nodes and the
blood. Thunder fists and is waving in the currenting
light and spreading appetite considers its options.
It's better to be forgotten.
Shake your body out into uselessness.
Lay your sweet head on the flex and the gaze-that-floats-us of
the rivers hoboing through the staring land.

And then, in the fucked, hillbilly motel, your
pubic hair going into the cave to coconutrug with others' pubic hair, the
curtain with its rod on the smoked television, the comforter's eight month
deisel smell, a line of R20 insulation on the table,
the ego can comb its beautiful hair and think of John Stuart Mill.
There are many versions of *Anne of Green Gables* on the television.

Non-Hodgkin's lymphoma, a heavy dark bird, bearded
like an old railway engine, Assyrian beard, lifts on farms over six
thousand acres.
What's happening a little way on in the beer parlour? They're celebrating
his decision to forget his decision not to drink.
It's possible to think of the perita of grass, bony assemblage, the
conciliar hum of erotic argument, steepling, unrolling over
days, adverbed by the moon fidgeting under purple-green slough ice.
All this takes a long time, the time of psalm cycles, a long sailing; begin
by sleeping near a grave. Stand back; look down.
The cafe is open two blocks away. We offer to cook our own breakfasts.
It's possible to think of the bones of things,
shark bone of argument, talk's bone ring, orchestral
raptor bone of rising speech going through you like a black wind.
Lymph of moonlight coming down the ancient canals.
Scarves of an encyclopedic muchness darker than this continent, this
at-the-moment.
Quick shapes of seeability, tongues coming out of things.
Everything is disguised, covered, everything is feathered.
The brown crust winter left on the windows.
The one neighbour you saw leaving the office the first night here you never
see again, black ball cap, his full, see-through bag of white bread.

1

Glaucon, the little slut, has taken in the *Iliad*, its streaming metal weather,
    diesel exhaust; he hooks his eyes into the muscling night,
    horses flicking fast on fire on the leaping beach, but
    not sat down to the *Odyssey*, its humming, flowing
teeth, it apokatastasis, the buffalo-jawed self-crumpling, the sleepwalking,
                    self-leaving wave,
and so, of course, heard nothing of the country inside his own
tooth, unknowing field, not smelled it, beach-damp stippling
into the room like fever lines, as North America was
smellable two hundred miles into the Atlantic,
the erotic life, empty spreading, gold-ringed, circled by a shimmering noise,
a this-only-this breeze scrimming its top, nor felt it lift like a
room of people, excited, in heavy clothes, and suddenly standing.

2

Leave ontology behind.
Leave goodness behind, said Socrates.
Take the drinkable pelican wave further into your mouth.
Until the blue desire appears standing on its feathered, python
tail, and you are speaking with it at a distance and cannot hear what
is being said, though this is soaking your beard and the skin of your face,

though a red tent, well-hipped, lowers itself over the talk,
and there are drownings going on, intimate to you, in the mouth
in front of you.

3

An illness comes up to you like an animal in symbolic clothes
from an unthinkable quadrant, a coyote
with a willow stick and a pointy hat, sprinkled with gopher dirt, and
tells you: a
breast embedded in a tree, a forehead
burbling from elm, marriage, here, with displacement, is possible.
He is speaking flesh, the animal that has been elected to
raise its left foot, to appear like a tree full of hearing sewn into
your thigh or lower neck, exactly where you are now.
Some hard thing, shot wrapped in leather, comes down, comes down,
over a rain time, over a long time,
and your bones crowd against the walls of the room.

4

The milky forehead of the secrecy of
beings – dead goldenrod, etc.
The turbine of things ignoring but
contiguous with other things:
the large blue wheel starting to move.

The large blue wheel starting to move. Anne Szumigalski dead and starting
out along the poplared axis mundi, in shiny Army and Navy
            shoes, in snowshoes, in a black ship,
seafoam scummed and the light river, the god, coming firmly toward
    her, its face of surf, and carrying her forward, with tall, white assertions
and erasings, and throwing her over the snow-
    pinned field, people waiting for her on the other side in bright trees,
                over there, in the bright trees,
                            moonfaced
buddha, sunfaced buddha.

I want to have come up in me a scintilla of idleness, speaking, animal
flash, like a swallowed tree
of cinnabar, like a complete city on a plain, Beijing, late
in the twentieth century, early December, workers' apartments in the west
of the city, a little snow, steel plants near, coal particulate
and mothballs, nearly supper, people inside starting
to cook, cilantro and tomatoes, imagine the climb of plumbing, lights on to
the top, someone inside reading *Smilla's Sense of Snow* in English, and
                                                  further back
throat-closed, wolf-remembered hills and monkeys and miles
of grown-in shrines where the nights have not been emptied in
years, so they spill over the sides.
You can smell the high snows of hiddenness here where I am, your feet are
          in the snowboat of loss.
There's a crawlspace under the talk, all the way through the
                              chokecherry thickets.
So there are small prints in the snow along the creek, Flying Creek,
in collapsing sun.
So there is monasticism, there is the part in Islamic
military science where they empty the country.
I can't begin to tell you how abject I am. This is two parts of a
darkened church bowing to one another, what they had
been chanting to one another in the dark, the dark, the goldmouthed
                              wall, going on.

II

THIS

The road goes through the eye.
The green breathing of this road makes it a truly *serious* Antonio Machado
    road, winter-walking, rain, ascesis, the dead young wife, rain-then-snow-
    then-rain, chimney smoke, rain and walking.
So: a religious road.
The doctor of emptiness that is also the gravel road east of Chauvin humping
                        past Suffern Lake and
    the jacklit, god-on-a-pin shack the colour of a snow-moth-eyed collie.
And also the two-truck-tire-track-through-excited-but-self-clasped-grass
apophaticism to the slough full of blue-winged teal
where there is no mouth but the prosthesis of a long
looking, the stride of a look, bending like a tailbone at the end
toward the breathing things.
All this but there is another way and it pulls.
The givenness, the extruded feast-likeness of
                        the bend
of poplars, which is a kind of weeping.
The night's smell of horses
        is another way.
Let me tell you again what I think.
The night writes the vita of duckweed
and lodges it in the blue codex below the ground
where it is read eventually by a slowly unparalyzing beetle
just before the new wasp eats it in the birth-hole.

And the beetle, gathering darkness' sheaves and the honey of darkness reads
        as well of the combed homelessness of dragonflies in the inner grass,
their Tang robes,
how they brought the sutras from the
west, one letter at a time, one
letter brought into (translated, inhaled as a horse drinks water)
                one body at a time,
                        all moving east in sweet, fixed winds.
The road goes through the eye.
We wait and we wait;
we wait.

I

Hidden, hidden, hidden, I
          was under the ground, counting stones, touching my face
with my hands. Saskatoons around me, a first sword. There was the
shouldered, learned, unknowing, bearded, unborn river, a black, wobbling
lift or speech, a hero's old arm; under the earth, a rippling eared
     deer, and an eared grebe's red eye – immense, floating
conversations conducted by contiguities under the earth – wolf willow with
                                        its hump of scent,
          under the roof of the hump of its scent saying nothing.
The world waited under the ground, an army.
All of hardness push-leaned its elbow onto the back of every mosquito
          in the slumped attentive place.
In the ground, my breath was far into my house, wintered-over leaves.
A man like a fish held a bright disc in his mouth, Socrates
                              holding Europe.
And the crow flying under the ground, which was the whole
                    of the underground, a gob of grass roots in its beak,
crutched along a buried valley.
And a thing swimming in its asleep-gold egg moved in thickening
                    circles in a slow cup.
I was quiet, my scholarship was gold and shit, I slept days.
The sun was a lamp of butter, it was
the half-circle of the mated pelican's bill, it would not

tell anyone about itself, it had taken low lake water from the northern
                              end, algae flaking down, into itself.
Everything would wait, the separate things
would be telling virginity-losing stories among themselves,
                              and then they would come back
to be what they were but with a bright, living, mental rope among them,
coming from their foreheads and passing into other foreheads.
I was tied under the earth with strips of willow and when I looked, there
were palm-sized constellations near me, an oar stroke across
                              a blood-carrying dark, dirty,
sedimented like Qinghai silver.
In the ground, my mouth open, my tongue out, an aroused blue.
No moving, no moving, no moving, a leaning
into things gathering summery muscle along its neck.

                              II

We crossed the Lemsford ferry just when hollyhocks were starting
                              to bloom in the towns.
Field flowers out were gaillardia, yellowclover, sunflowers,
                              baby's breath and shasta daisies.
At Estuary, abandoned since the twenties, another crossing further along,
a five foot block of cement with a quiet hole, the old safe of the Standard
     Bank, and in the hills mountain ash trunks down in the high deer
          trail coulees, gooseberries thick-necked over the clay creek,
the coulee shedding its pelt over the mucus of earth.

Forty foot wells in the town flats, cool, grass-tasting water and desert
plate cottonwood leaves where you walk, four houses, two
with cars in front.

The river was brown-roiled, bulled up by snow melt stumping down
from the late mountains in red July, a two inch rain in the
foothills, mostly snow, spruce jumping in the pig-foreheaded flow,
and in late photon pollen, the high flat butte, Bull's Head, lifting,
Asiatic, feathers in its throat,
blunt, snubbed butte, atopos, late day, latest July, near Empress,
Alberta, maybe a fasting place, maybe a buried house.
I will become one of them (an antelope).
The dark lantern of the Red Deer River was moving slowly.
The seal-headed ferryman said the river was high at 8,800 cu. ft. a second
but not as high as in '95 when it was 38,000 cu. ft. and humped the upper
guy cable (it quivering in black water, it standing up in black water) the
whanging, curly head of water.
There was no getting into the forks, smoky with unlikeness, fenced pasture,
hills tipping from their foreheads over.
A great bowing in things. I had been under the ground, counting stones,
touching my face with my hands. I was now the body inside
my body, asleep, smoke in my clothes. Gold in my mouth as
I crossed the ferry. The river
jerky in flood, shuffled in its way not knowing
where it was.
I have begun to write the Subterranean Theology, the Telluric Theology.
It will be a stone even in the ear. Here the mouth is islanded.

The Senlac sandhills, near the Alberta-Saskatchewan border, under the
four inch winter coat of soil, in damp sand, under caribou moss, with
turquoise, in that carefully built and uncodified
        light, a drawn man, made with white stones

who closes his salmon eyes under the ground, the stone-under-
water weight of things, yes and no,
passing over,
and he is flying under the ground, fixedly blue,
in the other direction, thin and old, blue to the horizon.
He wears the jewellery of not being thought of.
The mouths below the ground, the ritual standings holding a feather.
His mouth is full of the ochre of Nicholas of Cusa, maxima doctrina,
his chest a ship, 15th century, in a two month crossing from Greece,
its sail a poplar bonfire.
His name is the small ground nest egg in his mouth.
He goes into the bluff charge of what he can't know.
Just the man's teeth are intact,
his bones tattooed with streaks of old fires, he flies
under the ground, a quail glide, through the opening and closing
dirt.
The dirt is closed, the dirt is open.
The Battle River is close, he smells it and leaves the ground and walks
toward it, sliding himself under it, where a sweet idiocy opens in

him and he's wearing a shirt made of eyes and he sees a faint-for-him
muscle: there are no favourites
even though the animals may come toward us.

IV

I spoke to the thing wavering in my mouth, the true
animal with the small river face and the body of
a river's course that had my face. It looked out from the cloud-pelt
                                                        of stasis.
It's dark in this place, stones cup cigarettes and talk to stones.
I look down at the back of my hand and see a goose
                            passes just under my skin,
the goose, a little over water, no wing beat, early October, October 8,
  shallow north end of Last Mountain Lake, reed islands, shit-coloured water,
                                    eye curve of earth, clouds,
                                    then sunlight, then clouds.
It makes you sick, the old-Chinese light
                    of this a staining, out of skin and into speaking, a
                                    staining.
I had a hard-on.
Light was ascending and descending in what
        I saw.
It was the inside of stones that had come out, the mealyness, uncleverness
        in Siberian-faced aspens that had come out and walked alive.
It stood by the poplar that had come up through my tongue

at the back, the white, feathered tree pinning my tongue at the back.
You let cities go out of your body, cities seen from the air, one from
                              the front of the neck, one from the lower back.
They leave cavities. You collect some wood and start a fire in one
              of the holes out of the wind.
I fall asleep and someone puts the peppery tang of the aluminum slug
      of a mid-autumn snowfall between my upper lip and gums at the front
                    of my mouth. And I'm ready,
hunched flowingly toward the ground in a limp of sick-long sleep.

I was in the ground and the animal came to me wearing signs.
It came out of the water moaning in stone, and it turned toward
                              me and this was speech.
The animal nitrogen-burnt with suns, moons, initial, beribboned equations,
loose canvas, scenes painted on it, on its sides, hanging
from leather-laced poles along its spine,
the animal's sides jewel-embedded,
its sides and neck quick with tongues.
The worm of the river was on my arm. Under my tongue, the river
                              tattoo, the thicket tattoo.
The animal's large sides were assemblies rising in canyons to speak two
                    things, one from the cottonwoods, one from
                    the shade side of the canyon wall.
The animal came with the world.
The animal came with many people inside; inside it was a boat, carrying
                    many people over night water, a kind of creature.
Its sides were long walkings out onto the flats.
All I had there was grass.
I was lying down; the word of the river was under my arm, cupped
                              in my armpit and I was lying
down in blue grama grass.
The animal came with the self-polished things.
It could have worn old Spanish armour, it could have carried flags,
                    say the flag of St. George.
It had sides of catanyxis.

It carried a plaster mirror with gold letters on it.
It had sides of a no-speaking but a musical, half-weeping gravity.
It lay down near my head.
It uncurled its mind, nothing there, no smell.
It had a gold band round its head.
The animal came out of the west and you could hear it breaking through
    trees, a little later, moving east in insistent dark.

Throat steepled, blurred with variety, wild
licorice in flower two days after the feast of St. Benedict, small blue
dragonflies, auto-body blue, hooked almost mentally in a screwing which
is a tin-tin-tin-nabulation of pretty well unphysical bells; they are
eye-sewn to a stick poking from the water, Islamic shadows on the water.
Desire's work, I was slid under things and
saw the dusky words engraved on their belowsides.

A flag of names blows inside the tongue; in another
place a deer hunches back into chokecherries; there
is a wave inside the earth, the pelvis surfs on the black
roll and buck; let the hidden, shy, terrifying things
lift you in their long red beak.
A fox below the ground does his calculations,
        gold marks on a blue like someone saying yes, yes, yes, of course,
        that's it, a blue like seeing with the eye that sees you;
the fox's quick, streaking marks smell like the vaginal fluids of white
                                        women,
or like pelicans moving low on the water, almost touching the water, almost
    night, July, the water green, not aware of itself, unlike itself, alert.
The throat clouds with variety; it is two days after the feast
of St. Benedict, wild licorice in flower,
dragonflies entering domed rooms and the whirling of one another.
The fox sings the Fourth Gospel in tiny braille pricks of light-sound

that rise an inch and a half in weeds, a small fluid range of light.
In its jaw, the animal remembers the deep, black-almost-to-nonexistence, old
       sleepy violin of Heraclitus, the severe gong of what is required.
The world sits on the point of his momentumed concentration,
the fox of wheel, the fox of breath, of circles, the fox
of the breathing eyes in things;
it memorizes the blueprint of sorrow and motion set out for particular
people, and builds what this says by walking through it completely.
As the fox walks the route in another place, the occult order, cathedrals,
heroisms rise, deaths rise, selfishnesses rise, all the states, and they blow
back into you converting you into the wind of what they are.
The fox who could have been once a man, Abaris the Thracian, say, part
raven, part gold arrow, or Gregory of Nyssa, his monstrous, stupendous –
       Constantinopled, gold-walled, shouting, gliding – hybristic eye.

The fox below the ground
wears a hat and beats time with a stick thin as a merlin's scream
It reads its one book cover to cover, then again.
Lord Hermes, Lord Porphyry.

Sullen slow heave of Mars above whacked-down
                corn after supper,
the forest is not small, there are towers of
                    seeing,
old deer scaffolding, built close to it,
near smoke pillars from stubble fires,
and above and through it a smooth, deep-throated wheel
           of starlight and snowgeese you could take to the bank;
we open our mouths and the word is put in;
the lit skeleton of what is has walked into me;
now a runner's muscle of ice on the pond, thin as a swede saw
blade, now a coat of chickadees, coat of chapters
one and three, Book ii of *The Mystical Ark*, coat of looking-
until-you-are-poor no one wants but fits, moon thickening over, moon
thickening, eating something, its own arm, then going
down a back stairway.
Keep this to yourself and
smoke-carrying, matted Beaver Creek that is just beyond
your looking-away left hand.
You could reach it but it's always late
              in the afternoon and time for a beer.

Then inside *The Mystical Ark*, between chapters seven and eight,
Book II, on the contemplation considering the rational principles of visible
things, on its abundance, snow in the afternoon, a winter-coat deer, its
brief auric, moony huffing, three years old, shoulder cut, mule deer, pushing
north, it turns its one, restored head,
it lifts it front right hoof holding it back then awkwardly out,
it is hard to do this, and there is a folded paper
in the slot, a single word on it: *desire.*
Mars rising later, later, then losing interest, the moon
three-quarters through its manifestation, cupping an ear.
The animal has had to come up the cleft of the book and see
a solid, cruel-lipped fire.
It has passed through a shouting wall and various eschatological smells.
Ice quill-rattles on the river.
This also engines forward partway up the valley cliff, late
fall, crops off, stubble burnt, across the water from where dolphin-skinned
rich have built some houses with a particular form of light they've
found and they are calling in their dog.
Along a feeding creek an owl is bunting and yanking
out of a human face that grows a little way back on
as the owl's head continues to whip.
The water could lift up and walk out of itself in tall
bright hair,
it could move below a violent, instantaneous grove of hair,
     its secret body appearing.

WHAT XI CHUAN DOES, WHAT A LOT OF US DO

I

You fly under the ground, older, badly, through frost lines, unstrummable,
smelling the iron pockets, fish of the exigent-lit lowerland, long
grass across your mouth which is five years of silence, roughly
Pythagorean, five miles between church
and house, the water for the week to carry back, there
is the wild roaming of never being found.
If you are right in your head you burn the year's production of
baskets just after Christmas, the oratorical fire a swallowing
                                        walk into the sand,
                        you, Bubalis, the hairy-backed, the never-at-home.
In you, a feather guest, a furious leaping.
You fly where the poplar bush is upside down, dark between beaver ponds.
Small flames come off your hands as they move toward the lidless, thick,
unloud work, you shaving yourself further and further,
walking notch to notch down the sheening, spoken-to tree.

II

St. Ignatius of Loyola from three o'clock on on a December afternoon,
feather master, on a low pine-veneer bookshelf from Wal-Mart under
a light not strong enough to read by, inside his lightly buffed forehead
the sea off Newfoundland – even in the print

he is poltergeisted around by muscular dwarf
tears few see. Their pillow-lipped, shouldering mouths. His
leathery weeping for years.
Details propeller-blade around his eyes, he can't get around this.
The sleeve of beauty just brushes his neck and he's air-hammered into the
air four feet or somewhere else, slack-skinned, a stuttering wave of
                                            blond breath,
the tears always in him, a slope of birch, a scarlet hill,
the large nose inside his brain
breathing in, breathing in the light of Their Speaking
to one another as he presses his face to his mind and They,
Bright They, do not see him, not yet, do not
look his way, just yet.
You – there are geese like a small iced pond under your skin,
your hand, your shoulder points.
You don't know what to do. Keep walking.

III

Christmas, Beijing, a Santa with the skin of a dead mouse in front
of the Friendship Store, blindfolded hills slowly standing up
behind the steel plant plume, the government closes an exhibit at the
National Gallery, a little snow on the ground, spit marks, coal dust and a
market in Sanlitun favoured by foreigners and chic, mildly shimmering
Chinese, this haunting the one true mechanism, the rabbit-out-of-
                                            a-hatism here.

A lightly padded cold on Jiangomenwai.

You're in red shoes, a blue coat, sun through clouds a burnt aluminum
kettle bottom, walking toward the Five Flavours Tea Room, the medieval
observatory, star theatre, star laboratory, off the second ring road, full
of immense bronze seventeenth century Jesuit instruments, some willed
        straight into air, into which the fist particulate of not-quite-day, not-quite-
night is falling and hardening, gas and hot cooking oil
lifting through the traffic.

Xi Chuan, dressed in clothes he's thought about for a week, called toward
his face from a book, goes to the window in an apartment near
the airport and looks south.

And suddenly another world inside this world is herded along a dry, mum
road pinned by Lombardy poplars planted too closely together two days on a
no-holds-barred train ride deeper west.

1

The *only* way in is impoverishment. Don't repeat this to anyone. Everything
is poor, moving in a slow light from itself. Further in, a dark. This
is home and song. The names of things
are hidden and alone. Everything is sheared off, orphaned – the beginning
of wealth that doesn't imagine itself that way, the beginning
of desire. Desire, the plumed thing.
You could hear something *if* you could migrate into things.
The damage of cold lowers a rope with which you might be able to lift
what you are into the ash of things' burning, what they cast, what
follows them. Nothing cares for this. All desire
is here; all desire one desire. Everything is mortified: then all things
see.
There is a world next to the world and eros milks into it. It is the
clear field with its light inside and would appear if the fixed word would
come toward us out of the forest.
Nothing is more than this. The word,
the word can be said
to not exist. From desire, a garden would come.
An impossibility shines in things.
Intelligence, light and small things moving with queer deftness in
trees and grass.
Things are the speech of an untonguable darkness in themselves.

Things, which are the rest of us, the part
cut out, do not love us.
There is a sorrow and a sleep in things.
Something which is not here and which always will not be here
will speak for us, say the dark
matter in us. This, us, outside us, grows
a dense point in the hidden ground.
Geese on the river, walking the half-iced river, are our breathing
and our thinking: this, glinting spectacle of our breath, comes from the
larger dark of eternity. Where else
could you live but in a simple hole, listening?

2

Joan says Patrick, Patrick, Patrick is really a primitive artist
trying to have sleek through him with longlegged brightness
what can't come through, the bird
in the house with mirrors, swallowing, trying to have
                all of it, even its skeleton, in him then
through him, his mouth weird and wrongended.
(Shaved head, understone hands, his dog's smile.)
Everyone's being muttered through, she says.
P. dreams an ermine walks down
                a nursing home corridor
and bites her through the throat. She thinks she's
lost and loses half an hour driving home when her car

crosses the eyeless river.
Everything's being muttered through.
Today is first snow
               moving out over fields inside the stone of frost.

3

I started in the ground
and I brought nothing with me.
I came out, mouth covered, remembering.
The animals, night stones, lifted a curtain and I walked out
               through the grass and came along the wedge of creek, huddled
                                      light.
I was in a boat, it was night when I came
across, I was in the earth boat.
I came out and seeing was all over me.
               And I was covered with seeing.

4

Joan is writing about a woman in
               whose ear bees build their golden pueblos.
There is the wind of the mind in the grass.
The grass has my vote.
The grass is the beautiful city.

Because of where it's gone and what it's
        lost, its mirrors are like drinking pure alcohol.
All afternoon, along its walls, I'm loose, on the move, money in my pocket.
You must efface yourself if you are erotic.
Joan says its cause for amor fati Ukrainians
                        settled where they did near poplar
                thickets and sloughs in north-central Saskatchewan
because what's there sees their sort of singing completely, all
                        its weight, all its night.
Bony churches taking in the male and female callings, counter-
        callings, poplars nosing into a clear bunch the voice-damp churches.
In the grass, a stunning courtesy.

5

Let me tell you what I think.
Things began beyond the river in the white getting up of the hills, where
the light was inside itself, nothing
showing outside the light, beyond the river, this where it
started, past the herds moving and stopping, out there,
where the light was this resting in what it was and even
more was brought up fully (in-breathed, pulleyed) into its idea, then
not even there. It started out in that place, in that bowing inhalation.
Then it fell; an awkwardness in light
        and it fell.
The world appeared out of this.

A clumsiness golden with heirloomed light.
Coyotes move in the water-dark, back-of-the-eye dark valley, the
                afternoon light in the higher trees is a woman, looking.
None of this should be reported, leave
                it alone.
None of this or nothing at all
comes into the mind, an animal coming there. It does
                not come.
The world in any way in us – this is
                impossible – is tears. Weeping is thinking entering eternity.
With things your virtue doesn't matter.
None of this is for you.
Juniper is far, snowberry is far and hard.
Learned ignorance is all we put on the plate.
When you look into a distant thing as into a mirror, you
will see something that will terrify you.
Everything that is is both erotic
                and does not care for you.
It does not travel toward you but it moves; motionless, it moves.
Everything is rag-poor, light-poor, it moves.
When, because we are frank, buried, unlimited
widows, because nothing works, things come
toward us, when the river enters us then, it feels a little like a low-
                grade fever,
it feels a little like a lowgrade fever,
it feels as if we've just been missed by a car.

COULD BE FEB. 14, 1244, COULD BE NORTH JAPAN

Curved snow fields,
tracks thick, spreading,
gathering in whose ear?
Flying Creek, Rock Creek, Wolverine Creek, Beaver Creek:
                              hidden.
Manitou Lake (Neilburg), Manitou Lake, Quill Lake,
            Cabri Lake: salt straight through, all hidden.
Estrus, piss marks at the bottom of the drifts.
I am under the ground, moving
      my arms to the stars, the asthmatic mind of Tu Fu
four or five steps to the left, and an inch or
so further below.

III

The house, finally, is under topsoil and stones, lit with
      mind light, low talk, the given looks of animals.
A stove burns in it with the variety, the burly he's-got-a-knife stagger
                of the *Phenomenology of Spirit*.
Moths in the armpits of the house,
small blue moths around its mouth.
There's complete water here, water that doesn't think about itself.
The wingspread of the house, its owl-duskness.
All its iron lies outside.
It keeps its blood in silver boxes.
The house in its crouched and altruistic speechlessness is greatly adding
      rows of numbers, stupendously, big-handedly sewing together tendrils
                of numbers. The sum will be
the hidden king. What does the house
want of me? It's a bear
smelling winter, moving further back into the mountains,
shoulders thunderclouding through goldenrod.
The furbearing house,
a pelt of dusk, metal shavings on the back of its neck.
The walking house, the walking house.

You leave the gold-tongued, disastrous house,
and, erect or not, are on highway 2 south of Moose Jaw heaving
into the dry, escaped horse hills near Ardill, you're south of
Old Wives Lake, salt lake pong, road lit form below, buffalo lit,
one blood bell swung slowly under the earth, then angle down
into the paint-by-numbers capitalism of Assiniboia, a mouth of small,
tight teeth, coffee and cinnamon bun at the Peking Pearl restaurant,
and into first mind hill country south of Rockglen, fresh-legged
moon in the grass, then just before the border, pull off to the right, no
sign, an Appaloosa creek, and quaver over unawakened, wholly physical roads
west, late afternoon, sun wallow, you see everything, criminal country,
country that steps out of itself, country way back
in the mouth, right, left, then over the valley
lip, and there's Rock Creek, golden
eagle cliff, deer in the coulees, a little belly
and muscle with the here-and-there, moving light.
Last year's poverty is not this year's poverty.
Anomalous, in love with homelessness, desire.
Leave the truck. Work upstream along an old track, six o'clock
shade caving from the bluff over weed-haired water, just-
frightened deer moving back into grass like stars coming into place.
Trails around like pale multiplication tables in memory.
The antelope's stare when you're coming back will set up a small
homestead of thinking in you.
If you are lucky, you are going into exile. If your luck holds.

54

This Going to the Quill Lakes I wrap in a piece of blue wool
    and hide in the tool shed where the wasps have made a flowing
        flexed sensorium.
These wrist-thick dragonflies, Tartar dragonflies, this seeing of
    them a body itself, standing there, large, iris-nosed, interpreting, faintly
    and with additions, the words, part-words in things, I wrap
    in a piece of cloth and hide.
The mud house, the half-buried house, house with beams wavy like moth
    flight, a Saharan mosque, its pebbly walls, goes up into what
of itself it takes for an ear and arranges there an ornate being overlooked –
the dark stalks of the tongue fall
    under the murked erotic momentum of what is
entering light in the world, the fields of the tongue sinking under the
flowing shoulders of delighted ontic dark, the dark fields of the tongue
    lie down and gold books appear beneath them –
      Shobogenzu, Periphyseon, The
      Mystical Ark, Larry Levis' *Elegy.*
The dark fields of the tongue lie down and animals appear within them,
lying down like bombs near the head or lifting their forepaws in a hard
    but carefully psychagogic, Cappadocian way.
The dark fields of the tongue fall down in the push of what loves
and can't be said and does not care for us and there's nothing to say about
        this.
Night works into the tongue's fields, the red-blond speakings, and
the averted stalks lie down and stay lodged, gathering bits of music, bear-

running-like ideas, berries of shadow like small gymnasts under themselves.
I take off my clothes, let my hands go to
sleep at my sides and step down into the pool.
I don't know how long I will live.
I listen to the chiming dark, my forehead to that forehead.
I look into the night and read, read, read. The wasp
of the dark sucks smally at my face. This
is all I am good for.
The grass has a popeye forearm, it's efficient.
A blinding foot comes out of what has no
        names, Don't say this.
A speech which is like an unbearable nudity – Don't
    say this –
comes near but won't move through
    the wall; Don't say this.

Land around Dillberry Lake, black
bear waving through last summer, swaying, spored heat,
mosquitoes pilling and spouting, teeming shoulders of the bear
                          in a cleft northwest of the flat, rotting lake,
the sand colour of Pyramid Mountain lounging in the country
here, vacationing near Dillberry Lake,
the land around Chauvin, Edgerton,
along the Battle River, deep breath of it, Senlac a little
further west, shot sand roads, bird eyelid colour
of wolf willow, the pre-occupied bachelor hills there,
once you get into the country, eighty per cent sleep. The cafe
at Chauvin, good hamburgers, raisin pie, full of big women with
steam ploughing off them and quiet men floating in the small room.
The cafe at Senlac better yet, a crown of local brands along the
top of the wall (like the bar at Val Marie) and kids'
blue toys along one windowsill.
People pass through moving under the ground all the time here,
not herds of them but two or three every so often, people in their
late teens, older people from hospices in Edmonton, under the ground,
                        feathery with fishbone and carrying old water.
Water dark like the shut mountains north of Beijing, Red Snail Mountain
lifting just behind the abbot's room in the fifth century emptied
temple, its swallowed speaking bell, room with curvy, black, thick, eyebrow-
like beams and other mountains behind it with mouth-cupped shrines,

crazy bearded males-off-on-their-own places. Like the Dillberry Lake
area where otium sanctum flops back and forth like an eye-tipped
grass blade in the noses of a few animals.

I meet Louise, and I've got the Platform Sutra
of the Sixth Patriarch in the bag the Taoist nun at Xining told me
      would always feed me luck, the one with the yellow-green bird
streaming from mere being.
On the lefthand side of Hui Neng's book, old characters like the lost forest
      north of Chang'an, people moving in it, soft-mouthed older people,
          catching birds with long poles and string.
We go to see *The Apostle*, Robert Duvall.
In the film, Duvall has Motion balled in his hand: he looks at it then
             us, quickly, back and forth through the film.
Duvall's on a roll; what he's doing is rhythmic and ugly; he's
      always musical, bucking, but you can't be sure what you see
         inside. Sometimes a room that someone's just left,
            sometimes a garden of machines.
I want to write about human brightness coming into the world, out of
           the water in the ground and into the world.
Hiddenness appears in everything.
It lifts out of the chest of everything toward you, elm
      shade, wheat, a river, late grass.
Come in, it says. Where have you been?
You could say that when Louise and I sit
there watching the film we are being
thought by the dark.
It says what it needs to say.
The tongue casts its shadow but the mouth is bright.

SWALLOWED RITUALS

for Robin Poitras and New Dance Horizons

These are in the stone.
There is a fox's foot.
Snow is falling,
snow is falling,
widowed, broke, black-shelled March snow
dipping its shoulders into the pay-by-the-week motel of the doorless hills.
In the stone, there's a fox's foot hanging
                    from a wind-troubled, black wire.
There is an ocean in the stone,
        a mid-ocean there; it is breathing.
I'm sorry, I've said this wrong, it is Last Mountain Lake
        on a loud day that is there. You know that place.
The lake is a cup of hearing.
It hears the animals below the ground, the blur,
                    their shoulders pushing.
It hears the darkness, moving,
the muscle-sliding dark.
Go below the small things, I think, then
walk inside them and you have their kindness.
There is suffering and politics and the clay jawbone of a whale
        swaying left to right (be careful), right to left (careful) far
                                    in the stone.
There is the stone in the stone, conatus essendi.

60

There is Socrates curled in the coyote hole below the erratic of
        night, talking to a beautiful, light-pelted boy.
A camel train of cutlery goes by,
a mule train of hotel beds,
carrying bales of dried tears from the blind valley (they smell of kelp),
the interior, from the grassy place between the lakes.
There's a white foot serene with bones, there's a light.
When Henry Kelsey died or left Hudson Bay, he started
a walk below the ground; first he was just an inch below, then the grass
came to his shoulders, then he was gone inside, this was the
                kenosis of Europe: all he was
then was his voice, the upper part of it; he walked under the Swan River
and under the big forest north of the Saskatchewan near what was later
Somme and started moving west below the Porcupine Hills, working
down the muttered, water-necked slope.
He was a voice, the house of a voice, but nothing
was in it and he wanted someone to put a shining glide in his mouth, he
wanted some low drift stitched there, a late afternoon standing up of dust
from a dry year.
He found smoke and blue foreheads of pooled groundwater. He got thinner.
He built many irresistible lean-tos
        for his ear, spruce boughs, driftwood, space debris.
Later he died a second time.
These ceremonies can't be seen because they live in the lazy cheek and
in the thigh curve of mathematics and in the stream hump
of music, as Pythagoras said they did.
If you find one, if one comes up to you on naked brown legs, let me know
and we'll kill an ox together in delight.

The communal hot water footbath in the stone,
      the familia in the stone,
not the night and the push of the North Atlantic,
not the fur-backed water north and inland, the exposed
spine of its bright unfolding,
but the sung trees,
the sourire at the tip of this frozen coyote shit,
Descartes alone in his poêle, the waxy, meadow-flavoured room, inside the
speech of dreams coming likely from another head, so, then, D. inside a
tighter, more personal room,
Gilbert of Hoyland licking the unuttered breasts,
the ray-wounded mouth of John of Ford,
the moving, deer-shaped mouth of John of Ford.
Muscled ice already just sitting there in the reeds
below the train bridge, the golden eyes swimming and slivering into the
confessed, bare-shouldered current,
first week of December, snowing, a day after freezing rain,
the pingue otium of the river sleep-curving into the too-dry-to-freeze clay
cliff, the nose of seeing runs along this and smells
the chest smell of a loved animal; everything shunts toward the fire.
John of Ford had a longliving deer-shaped mouth,
his lips were herds moving at dusk.

Plato is talking with John Scotus Eriugena; a young woman, asleep in her
back of the throat body, from a class in advanced poetry; Julian of Norwich,
with her neck-bell of blood; Isaac of Stella and *The Cloud of Unknowing*;
they've come in off the range for the night and are under the ground,
whickering orange-winged grasshoppers around them,
dust, an angry stray dog, a buffalo-scented, mudfooted moon.
They have a fire going behind the windbreak of the hood of a '74 Plymouth
Fury ii. In P.'s throat are the whip lines of ten thousand snowgeese
                                                    two months away.
Transfixity has come and embedded itself in their ribcages; this is
the enacting, the being, of a weeping, sitting around a black fire,
talking. The fire burns with no light, pulling the wings and torsos
of all light into it, even the light of what is being said right now.
Late, late August, the edge of the world, the backs of the moths
heavy with eyes, the mosquitoes can't get to the talkers
so far below, the blue clouds grind against the earth.
The imagination has burnt down around their ears, they are ashamed.
Everything would fail in a way no one would notice without this.
Corn is in tassel in the gardens at night, one art.
They're here for just six hours, then gone, some into stones,
some hauling freight north of Whitehorse,
not shaved, poundingly confused.

Romanian Christ moon, full of bees, full of sweat-hard shirts,
                                its smell of mouse shit in an abandoned
shack, an abandoned shack, the moon's face a ton of China-shipped grain,
mid-ocean, insomnia-blackened with weed seed, moon where
a hundred sit down to eat in a hockey arena above paper tablecloths and say
nothing (it's a funeral), peeled moon, mosquito moon, moon with water of
mosquitoes and bosomy spear grass, light of vetch and illness, the creek-
deeper-than-it-is-wide moon, its look
a two-armed cradle of bony passageways,
a sheafholding of places to squirrel into, to stand up alive
in, hiddennesses, rotten trunks to not eating stand in alive,
whiskered light shafts where your life will be spoken into your face.
Let the one for whom this is meant make a church not only of
                desires but also of thoughts.
He should leave an ear with a tree
because he's had a place made for him for the waiting with heat lines
                                coming off of it.
He will find blackberries and saskatoons heavy and bull-tongued
        inside himself where there should be speaking,
and he will wait with the waiting that has June lines of slowness and
                                lounging
and fat hearing coming off it.
The moon with its rotted cardboard and deer-pissed-on grain
smell, the moon's old linoleum and the
sorrow, sorrow, sorrow, sorrow stroked into the ancient cutting board.

64

The coneflower moon, the yellow clover hovering
                              weight
stuttering through seen-by-no-one-but-swallows and by them
exegesised differently, lightly purple clouds,
then grazing out of them, rubbery weight gathering to the shoulders and
back, wasting time, what a gorgeous piece of golden shit, this moon.
Underground streams that are a kind of speech you listen
to by inhalation and exhalation are around here, thinking
of foot-high armies on horseback, thinking of the human heel
fountaining into the human ankle.

The dead clover climbs out of itself,
out of epaulettes of snow and out of
the wind which it knows both kataphatically and apophatically and
walks around the ledge of its
body as if that thing were a tall building.
Reptilian, lightly feathered with ekstasis, stunned it can
do this at all, it shines with looking, looking,
and with moving its small bright head.
The small dead clover lifting itself like a calf smelling the udder
to speech and walking out of tufts of snow.

Large, black-bear-on-its-back-legs quiet down where
the snow humps a little and bends as if it were
trying to assist or pass a note to the ice that performs
the ceremonial work of staring at the river.

The animals gather, their hoofprints
in the snow on frozen Beaver Creek, the moonless second day
after the story of Carol Shields' cancer appears in the newspaper.
Days later, I'm talking with Celestine about the problems she's
having with her boyfriend; I tell her I'm helplessly
reading John Cassian and what he says is a poplar-scented
and lit ship, very quick.
I get into it as it slides through the cold air ten feet up but the way

ahead is harder than the first 100 pages of *The Philosophy of Right*,
    mountains stepping from disguises in the distance,
                    yet it is still very fast.
It's going to the fluid Dark that drinks you deliciously.
Inside the breathed-out flame of eros, the heavy-lidded flying is a face.
                    It is a face.
The dead clover walking from shoulder boards of snow
and speaking. It is a face.

Tracks, deer slots, are gathering in my ears. I have
many enemies.

so

Everything takes a religious pose.
Everything appears in the passenger seat of a round-shouldered Datsun
    quarter ton, dying red, bones on the dashboard, in crane-backed light,
    and going south past the White Cap reserve, chuckwagon circle, sports
grounds, red willows where tart baskets rise like floppy hands, shacks
and trailers of golden-lab-faced bachelors, shaving now as
we speak, combines stripped down in the yard, someone passing through,
sleeping in a school bus, helping a few days, young guy whose life like a lazy
eye doesn't look straight at you, the road moving slowly from side to side
down, smoke from the bus undressing upward, the stack welded just behind
the black mirror; everything stands up in itself
on a hydraulic of light.

And I'm in the ground somewhere around here, late September morning
clouds – colour of trout skin, colour of trout flesh – smoothing over, east
to west, a degree over frost, my body in my eye, the eye
waving like a flag, the earth way down in its chest, cities
lifting and falling in the breath, teeming, braided, fluent, the red
faint keel along the bottom of the wind tipping a little and trembling,
diesel throb of migrations over the next hill and the next,
inconsequence in its grass nest, the slowly raised eyelid of the place,
cowpaths into and out of poplar circles, trees smelling of cow –
we come toward the Animals whose true, confessed bodies in diaspora are a
clenched, parade-like amnesia toward us, mule deer, white tail
billowing with weirdness and specificity, with our jumping, charge-heavy

voices, rocking, rocking;
when they come near us, they come near us through the grass.
Helen says the farms here are fucked. Some
have loaded a few bags and headed north, finding a way through
the thickets along the old oxbow ridge, crawling a way under snowberry,
rose and getting up and walking.

NOTHING SHOULD BE SAID ABOUT THIS

Basin Lake, scooped out, stripped to its shorts, crane's
bolt-hole, set aside, grass body odoured, pectoralled with nothing, early
                                                        May moon, feast day of
Athanasius and the beginning of the slab-foreheaded stability of Nicea,
                                                        green-flared
whitish-violet ice on the to-the-east Lake Lenore, wind thump-whacking it
to the north, nude low cliff, moon after lunch half-rotted over left behind
Basin Lake, alkali old man talk mark
around the water, heron blue-coasting over winter-killed reed, buffed
winds now from the north, grass almost migrated into fire, buffalo-
bean earing out of the ground, air colour
of dead heel skin, snow just gone from the trees, some drifts still
on north-facing hills; primum essence
living like in a motel inside the small unpainted house inside
goose skin and it doesn't move or say hello; horse smell of burnt grass,
a wind from the south with intent, propane thighs.
The ghosts go through the quivering world and pass through one wall here,
colour of toenail, the thin light bones,
sharp, that live in these parts go through.
Put your ear to the ground, everything is falling.
There is no hatred of philosophy here; stand by the bluish mud
along the shore and a new sort of citizenship comes
up, lashing its blinding tail.

GOING BACK; NOW, GOING BACK

The cupped, skinned-over, yellow
life below this life, the torso
unmarked by the claw of Origenist flame, ungrazed by the
flame and whump of large falling, that one, that
one, the one the ear settles on:
Manitou Hot Springs, dragon
seethe bumbling off the water, the water sick-slack,
in stained love with the sick, water with eyes
everywhere, under wings, at ankles, behind the ear, scrapes
you down to it, the breath-skinned, seal-like life,
which is thinking's sway, which is also fish-like, choiceless.
The sun disced palm of beauty carves you down.
Thirty-three below, Ski-Doo tracks
on the lake, medicine wheel
forgotten past the northwest
shore: stars smoothing into
thereness on grease of greater light:
rumble, inner ear problem of 5:00 p.m.
sun on owlheaded snow mounds
across unnameable ice,
the perfect hearing
of the axe-split moon hurting up through highbush cranberry.
Look down.
Something will begin,
        then pull itself back, it will really begin.

Dig a little way into the idiotic ground in a west-facing hill
at the edge of the Senlac sandhills, close to the Alberta border,
take this digging as your body, your turned-so-the-thin-side-shows
body, light's emigration clothes, you'll have to walk in
from the road for this, what you're doing is an old piece of deer scaffolding
left behind in poplar, hood the hole with willow branches before they've
leafed out, small sticks,
and crawl in, night will sway through where you are, leaving
a stain. Winter's shrugged off.
There's a coyote further back, eaten from the ass right through,
tail untouched, perfect flesh.
Bluebirds are a breath or so
    from being back.
Patches of snow like rash,
blurry moths pulsing over them.
Lights are going out in the Beijing-of-the-fifties hotel halls
    of thinking, Stalinism with chandeliers.
Even the stones are weeping, not in a
big way, but so small it's almost
sleep, almost the hair of sleep weiring
                over them.

Tusks of low aspens on the railway embankment in cold
April twilight, they hear
something.
They hear first ice below old ice,
sour ice in its who-the-fuck-cares otium sanctum; fish-flicker
of traffic under the ground; manure on the trails; the uncial
of the marsh hawk's head said and said, and below its undercarriage,
pasque flowers.
They listen to the unmapped ear in the hill, things passing around it,
                                        holding away from it.
I want the other ear, the dark one that floats under the ground
caught in unanticipatable breezes.
        It is
        the house that tall unlikeness walks into,
        the house where things bring their mum names
            in blue bowls, ringing,
        the house where night comes in and speaks in her long
            sung robes.
Hearing leaned against hearing, roofless, heavy wind,
almost all snow, snow dark as tooth rot, gone.

I am in the boat of John Cassian's mouth,
       night-coloured, mind-steered, poplar-scented, aspen-lit
ship, old limestone boat, dead ferns pressed into its side. This must
be kept a complete secret, hide it in the fat of your upper right arm.
We are running out of Egypt, holding fire, in paradiso,
burning locks of grass, great in the current, green there, the current a
hump of an animal beneath us, running us out of Africa.
       But soon he leaves me and I am passing through a rabbit scrub place,
antelope field, Bow Valley east of Hay, north of the
confluence with the Oldman, lower jaw valley, the bone of it, the lying-
out-in-the-open-of it, eight or nine feet up
in the uttered boat, ribcage anchor dragging along the tops of the grass
showing above snow, storm purpling in, the No. 1 highway starting to
                              close, the end
of the will in these parts, just long grain trucks dundering through in
                                heavy snow.

And this place is in the stomach of the thing,
and it is low in the breath.
The eyes in the willow, this willow,
    open.

❧

Somewhere in this terrain, this going about,
is an abandoned airplane hangar and inside it 10 or 15,000 square feet

74

of suspended tears, some close to the floor, some higher, the air
in the hangar the colour of snowberry thicket along any river east of
the Rockies, west of Lake Winnipeg, early winter, most of the angle iron
twisted, asleep, open along one wall.
Stephanus marks along the side of the tears. Work
your way through the tear field and you
will thin right down and see.
Nothing else can be read in this way; you must
read, read – work the shovel: go through
the tears, pry under them, the garden under the stone.

Listen, listen.
Three years ago, when the gold animal appeared to me,
a small combed sun, thin road, and took my smell,
it walked out of the robes of its custom
and it bent and took my smell.
It came very quickly out of the trees from the palmed night place, the
west, the labour-field, and lay down in the fire of my smell, leaning into and
half crumpling my tarp, its head hammering toward my shoulder and chest.
I was sick then, remembering badly.

AFTERWORD

Chipping sparrow, clay-coloured sparrow, sounding – you are stretched out in poplar duff, late spring, morning.

I wish to thank Peter and Louise who led me to Joe Cardinal. I also wish to thank Don and Jan for many years of deep friendship, and Helen for her fine ear.

I thank the Canada Council for the Arts for financial assistance. Some of these poems previously appeared in *Fiddlehead*, *Grain*, and *Poetry Wales*. "Kill-site" was published as a chapbook by Jackpine Press. Thanks to the various editors involved.

The quotation from Osip Mandelstam appearing as an epigraph is from *The Voronezh Notebooks*, translated by Richard and Elizabeth McKane. The lines from the *Odyssey* beneath it can be found in the Richmond Lattimore translation.

Non precor ut redeam
– Ovid, *Tristia*, II, 183